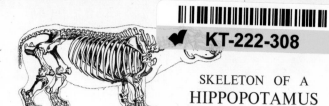

SKELETON OF A
HIPPOPOTAMUS

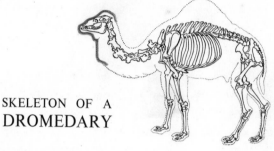

SKELETON OF A
DROMEDARY

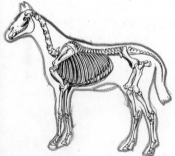

SKELETON OF A
HORSE

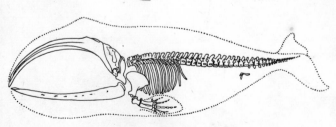

SKELETON OF A
WHALE

Series 651

The horse has grown the best kind of feet for running. The hippo likes to wallow in a warm river, so it has grown its eyes and ears on the top of its head, and its nostrils on the top of its nose. Cats, large and small, are night hunters, so they have eyes for seeing at night.

Facts like these are explained in this book about MAMMALS. It is not just a book about animals, it is much more; it is the story told in simple language, of how animals live, and how they have evolved to suit their way of life. It is, in fact, a book about the evolution of mammals.

The subjects include Hooves and Paws, Claws and Teeth, Tusks and Horns, Eyes, Ears, Noses, Voices and Tails. Twenty-four pictures in full colour illustrate this fascinating story of the world of animals, tame and wild.

ANIMALS
and how they live

by
F. E. NEWING, B.Sc. *and* RICHARD BOWOOD

with illustrations by
RONALD LAMPITT

Publishers : Wills & Hepworth Ltd., Loughborough
First published 1965 © *Printed in England*

MAMMALS

Everything can be divided into 'animal, vegetable or mineral', as in the game. The animal we mean is any creature which can move of its own free will, including birds, fishes, reptiles and insects. When we speak of animals in the ordinary way we really mean *mammals*, which are all the animals which produce their young complete, and nourish them in infancy on their mothers' milk. This book is about those animals, the mammals.

There are, however, some mammals which lay eggs. These are the duck-billed platypus and the spiny ant-eater, or echidna, both of which live in Australia. They are classed as mammals, even though they do lay eggs, because when the young are hatched they are fed on their mothers' milk.

The platypus is a strange animal, with webbed feet and sharp claws, and a broad beak like a duck's. It is a good swimmer and lives in burrows in the banks of rivers and ponds. It digs a very long burrow for its young, and puts up obstacles against enemies.

The echidna also lays eggs and then rears its young on the mother's milk. The mother puts the eggs into her pouch where they hatch and the young live until they can fend for themselves. The narrow beak-like mouth contains a very long tongue which darts out to pick up the ants on which it lives.

4

7214 0123 6

ECHIDNA

PLATYPUS

THE EVOLUTION OF THE HOOF

Over immense periods of time, animals have adapted themselves to the way they live and to the places where they live. They have grown the kind of feet, claws, jaws, coats, eyes, ears and even stomachs which suit them best. This process is called *evolution*. A good example of evolution is the development of the toe-nails of the extinct eohippus into the hooves of the horse.

The eohippus lived between fifty and seventy million years ago. It was about the size of a small dog, it ate grass and it ran across the plains. The fact that it *ran* is important. It had four toes on the front feet and three on the back, and being a runner it grew hard toe-nails.

The eohippus became extinct, but its descendants continued to develop the toes for running, and had three toes on each foot, with the middle one, on which they ran, longer than the others. Over countless generations the outer toes stopped growing and eventually disappeared, because they were not used, but the strong middle toes became hooves.

The horse, donkey and zebra are descendants of the long-extinct eohippus, and they have strong single toes or hooves, which are ideal for an animal which wants to run fast.

HORSE

HOOF OF HORSE — DEVELOPED FOR RUNNING

EOHIPPUS — ANCESTOR OF THE HORSE

HOOVES AND FEET

Just as the toes of the extinct eohippus evolved into the hooves of the horse, so other mammals have developed special kinds of feet. Cows, sheep, goats, deer, antelopes, giraffes and others evolved two toes with strong nails, which we call cloven hooves. Other mammals, including pigs, elephants, rhinos and hippos, have developed small hooves, or very strong nails, on all their toes.

All the mammals which have hooves are called *ungulates*, which is the largest family in the order of mammals. They eat grass or leaves and do not need to hunt other animals for food, and nearly all have good legs and strong hooves so that they can run away from the enemies who hunt them. Each kind has developed the legs, feet and hooves which suit it best.-

An ancestor of the camel had hooves, but the camel needed something special for travelling across the soft sand of the desert. So it has evolved a special kind of foot. It has two toes on each foot, with wide soft pads. When a camel puts its foot down, the toes spread sideways making the pads into broad flat feet which do not sink into the soft desert sand.

The llama of South America is a close relation of the camel, but as it lives in mountainous country and not on sand it has not needed to develop the special foot of the camel. Llamas are smaller than camels, and their special trick is to spit violently at any attacker.

MOUNTAIN GOAT

COW

ELEPHANT

DEER

WILD PIG

RHINOCEROS

CAMEL

CLAWS AND TEETH

We have seen that the animals with hooves are called ungulates. Another large family of mammals are the *carnivores*, so-called because they live mainly on meat. They are hunters, and their weapons are their claws and teeth.

The Cat family is an important branch of the carnivores, and this includes, with others, the lion, tiger, leopard, jaguar, puma, lynx and both the wild and the domestic cat. These have a special kind of claw, called *retractile*, which can be withdrawn or put out at will. Watch your cat at home and see how it can sheath or unsheath those sharp curved claws.

All the cats, large and small, catch their prey by springing on them, holding them with their claws and killing them. Whether it is a cat with a mouse or a lion with an antelope, the method is the same. To do this they must have sharp claws, and if these were not retractile they would soon be blunted. Sharp claws are important for the cats for another reason, they help them to climb trees.

The only member of the cat family without retractile claws is the cheetah, but as it is the fastest animal on earth it does not need sharp claws. A cheetah can run at sixty miles an hour. Instead of pouncing on its prey it chases it until it is exhausted and can be killed easily.

Carnivores all have very good teeth, with a pair of long sharp ones on each jaw called *canines*, specially designed for biting and tearing meat.

LEOPARDS

LION'S JAW

CLAW
RETRACTED

CLAW
EXTENDED

CLAWS, TEETH AND JAWS

The wolves, dogs, foxes, hyenas, bears and other mammals in their group cannot retract their claws to protect them in sheaths, because they are not used as weapons. Instead these mammals, which are also hunters, have strong jaws and teeth, including the two pairs of extra long ones called *canines*, or 'dog-teeth'.

Wolves and, in the wild state, dogs, hunt in packs and chase their quarry until it is tired out, when they kill and share it among the pack. The fox hunts alone, and uses its speed and cunning to catch its prey.

The hyena has very strong jaws and teeth, for a particular purpose. It does not hunt its own prey, but prefers to take the easier course of taking the leavings of some other carnivore, perhaps a lion. There may not be much meat left when the lion has finished, but the hyena can use its very powerful jaws to crack the large bones and get its meal from the marrow.

Bears keep their claws sharp even though these are not retractile, because they walk on the soles of their feet, as we do. This means that the claws are not blunted and can be used as weapons with the teeth, to kill and tear the meat. Bears are carnivores, but they also like sweet fruit and honey, and, when they live in zoos, buns and treacle.

WOLF

DOG SHOWING
CANINE TEETH

HYENA

DOG'S PAW

BEAR'S PAW

DIFFERENT KINDS OF TEETH

As we all know, lions and tigers are very fierce, but so is another group of mammals which are much smaller. These are otters, weasels, stoats, ferrets and mink. All of these are hunters and so have strong jaws and sharp teeth. They have lithe bodies, short legs and move gracefully and swiftly.

Otters live on fish, so they are good swimmers and have their feet partially webbed. The ferret is a relation of the stoat and is trained by man to hunt rabbits in their burrows. All animals which live by hunting have canine teeth.

The *rodents* are not carnivores, or meat-eaters, so they do not have canine teeth. Instead they have evolved teeth more helpful in eating their kind of food—grass, roots, nuts and, some of them, insects. These special teeth are long, sharp and chisel-shaped, and grow in the front of the jaws. These teeth are useful for cracking nuts and for gnawing through wood or taking the bark from trees. The rodents include rats, mice, rabbits, hares, squirrels, beavers, hamsters and porcupines.

Squirrels like nuts and they store them in the autumn to provide food in the winter. The squirrel holds a nut in its paws and bites through the shell with its strong chisel-like front teeth, and you know how hard a nut-shell is.

GREY SQUIRREL

STOAT

TEETH AND STOMACHS

Animals with hooves, the ungulates, live on grass, leaves and a vegetable diet, so they do not need the sharp flesh-tearing teeth of the meat-eaters, the carnivores, nor the long sharp front teeth of the rodents. Instead the ungulates have fairly sharp teeth in front, and flat chewing teeth at the back. They also have a strong tongue to help them eat grass.

A vegetable diet is sometimes difficult to digest so some of the ungulates have evolved a special kind of stomach. These mammals are known as *ruminants*, and include the ox and cow, the goat, sheep, deer and giraffe.

The stomach of a ruminant is divided into four separate parts and if you watch a cow feeding you will see how she digests her food. She tears the grass with her square front teeth, scoops it up with her tongue and swallows it without chewing. It passes into the first part of her stomach, where it is partially digested and turned into balls of cud. With a strong muscular movement she brings the cud back and chews it, using her flat back teeth. That is why her mouth moves sideways.

When the cud has been chewed sufficiently she swallows it again and it passes to the second, third and fourth parts of her stomach, where the digestion of the food is continued. The other ruminants eat in the same way.

COWS FEEDING
AND DIGESTING

UNGULATE

CARNIVORE

RODENT

VARIETIES OF TEETH

TUSKS AND HORNS

An animal lives by its teeth, using them for eating and fighting. The carnivores have very sharp teeth, the rodents have sharp teeth of a special kind for gnawing, and the ruminants have biting and chewing teeth. There is yet another kind—the tusks of the elephant, hippopotamus, walrus and wild boar.

Tusks, like other teeth, help an animal to collect food and they can be weapons, especially the tusks of the elephant and wild boar.

The elephant has the longest tusks, the record being eleven feet. There is a theory that an elephant's tusks are not only for gathering food and fighting, but to help to balance his great weight and bulk. Tusks are made of ivory, and to obtain this valuable product great numbers of elephants and walruses have been killed in the past.

Horns are also used as weapons. They are made of different substances in different species of animal. The horns of cows, sheep, goats and antelopes grow from the skull and are a covering, or sheath, over bone. Horn is a similar material to our finger nails, or the hooves of ungulates.

The giraffe has two small horns covered with hairy skin. The rhinoceros has one horn on its nose which is made of very coarse bristles matted together to form a very strong and dangerous weapon.

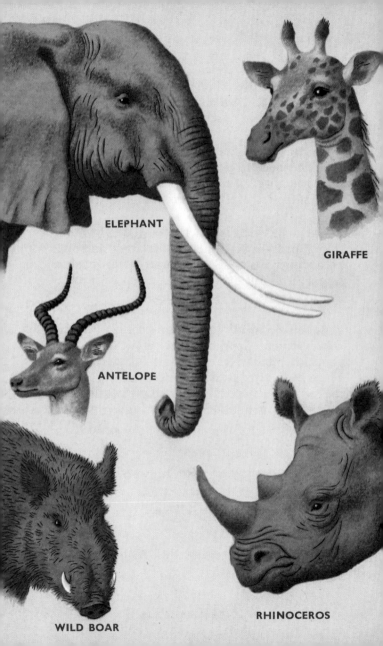

ELEPHANT

GIRAFFE

ANTELOPE

WILD BOAR

RHINOCEROS

ANTLERS

Branched horns, which are called antlers, are the main weapon of the deer family—the deer, reindeer, caribou, moose and elk. Antlers are only grown by the males, except in the case of the reindeer and caribou.

Antlers vary in size; the roe deer has quite small ones, while the much larger red deer often grows huge antlers, branched with many 'tines', as the points are called. Both of these deer live wild in Britain.

The antlers are shed each year, and in this they differ from horns, the new antlers grow larger, and often with an additional tine. So if you see a fine male deer, or stag as it is called, with six tines on each antler, you know it is at least six years old.

Antlers begin to grow in early spring when two soft velvety knobs appear, which grow quickly, and in about six months the stag has a full spread of antlers. These are covered with a soft sensitive skin, and we say the stag is 'in velvet'. This is to protect the baby deer, or fawns, from a jealous male; its antlers are too sensitive to use so the fawns are safe. Later, when the fawns have grown up, the skin dries on the stag's antlers and gets rubbed off, and he then has his fine strong antlers for the rest of the year, until they are shed.

The elk of northern Europe and the moose of North America are the largest members of the deer family. They have very large antlers, which are flattened or *palmated*, so called because their shape is like the palm of a hand.

RED DEER

ROE DEER

PALMATED ANTLERS
OF ELK (OR MOOSE)

EYES

Animals which hunt and feed by night have evolved specially sensitive eyes so that they can see when there is only a little light. Some people believe that cats can see in the dark. This is not so, they cannot see in absolute darkness, but they do need much less light than we require.

All the cats, great and small, and foxes, too, have slit-shaped pupils in their eyes which automatically grow large when there is not much light, and become narrow when it is bright. Dogs have eyes like ours, with round pupils, and these also become larger when there is less light.

When we meet a cat or dog at night we often see their eyes shining, as though they had lights inside. This effect is caused by the light reflected from the back of their eyes.

Rabbits and hares are timid animals much hunted by others, so they have evolved protruding, or 'pop-eyes' near the top of the head. This enables them to see all round, even behind, so that they can see an enemy in good time and bolt.

Hippos have also evolved eyes near the top of the head, but for a different reason. They spend most of the time almost submerged in the rivers and swamps of Africa, but need to keep their eyes out of the water.

TIGER

HARE

HIPPOPOTAMUS

EARS

Because the hippo spends so much of its life submerged in water it has also evolved ears on the top of its head. Over countless centuries animals have evolved the most suitable ears for their particular way of life, and for the place where they live.

Animals which are normally hunted by others, such as the rabbit, hare and deer, have developed large and very sensitive ears to give them early warning of the approach of an enemy. In the same way the animals that hunt them have developed sharp hearing to help them find their prey.

You can buy a special whistle which seems to make no sound when you blow it, yet a dog can hear it. The pitch of the whistle's note is too high for human ears, but it is clear to the sharper ears and hearing of the dog. As well as being able to hear notes too high for the human ear, a dog can hear sounds too distant for us, and it can tell the direction of the sound.

As with dogs, so it is with other animals. Hearing is part of an animal's equipment necessary for its life—for getting food when it is a hunter, or for being warned when it is hunted. Watch an animal when it is listening, and see how alert it looks, and how it 'reads' the message the sound gives it.

CAT AND MOUSE
HUNTER AND HUNTED

DEER

VOICES

Animals have an elaborate system of 'speaking' to each other, though not, of course, with any form of words. But they do use their voices to communicate with each other. One of the most awe-inspiring sounds in nature is the lordly roar of the lion, proclaiming its sovereignty over the wild. The same lion will purr with contentment when it is happy, just as its cousin, the domestic cat, purrs in front of a good fire or on friendly knees.

Two tigers hunting together will work some distance apart and keep in touch with grunts, growls and roars. A pack of wolves will call to each other in the excitement of the hunt, or howl to give vent to their feelings. A fox will call to another across the night countryside with sharp barks.

Animals do not chatter for the sake of it, they are too busy hunting or rearing their young. An exception, perhaps, is the monkey; wherever there are many, in a zoo or a forest or jungle, there will be tremendous chattering. Some monkeys howl and whoop, apparently for the fun of it.

The easiest way to hear animals 'talking' is to listen to them with their young. We have all heard the bleat of a lamb and the baa of the ewe, the high-pitched moo of a calf and the deep answer of its mother, the squeal of piglets and the grunt of the sow, especially her contented grunt at the feeding-trough. We know the horse's neigh and whinny, and the extraordinary voice of the braying donkey.

FOX BARKING

**DONKEY
BRAYING**

NOSES

Just as a dog can hear far-away sounds, so it can smell distant scents. The sense of smell is another vital part of an animal's equipment, and it is usually highly developed. Hunted animals are warned by their noses, as well as by their ears, of the presence of an enemy. The hunter uses its sense of smell to find its prey, and to track it down.

We know how keen an animal's sense of smell is from our pets. A dog can recognise someone by his scent. As we remember a person by his appearance or perhaps by his voice, a dog will sniff, and will remember him from its scent-memory.

As with the other parts of its equipment, an animal evolves the kind of nose it needs. The hippo has grown its ears and eyes on the top of its head, and its nostrils on top of its nose, for lying in water. Camels and seals can close their noses; they do it in the same way but for different reasons. The camel closes its nose against the blowing sand of the desert, and the seal against the water in which it spends most of its time.

The most notable nose of all, of course, is the elephant's. The nose and upper lip are joined to form the long trunk which the elephant uses as an arm and hand. An elephant can uproot young trees with its trunk, lift things, put food into its mouth or give itself a shower-bath in a river.

ELEPHANTS USING THEIR TRUNKS AND TUSKS

DOG FOLLOWING A SCENT

TAILS

With tails as with everything else, different animals have different kinds according to their needs. Man's very distant ancestors had tails, but these have long disappeared because they were not used. All that remains is a small triangular bone at the base of the spine, called a coccyx.

The kangaroo family have large, strong tails which make a tripod with the hind legs, so that the animals can sit up. Monkeys use their long and supple tails as an extra limb in the tree-tops. The squirrel uses its bushy tail in the trees, too; as a 'rudder' during leaps through the air and as an aid to balancing when running along a branch.

Beavers thump the water with their flat tails to warn other beavers of the presence of an enemy, and the rabbit uses its small white 'scut' to guide its young to safety. Otters use their tails as rudders when swimming.

Horses and their kin use their long tails as fly-whisks, and two horses will stand head to tail to whisk each other's faces to keep the flies off. We all know how a dog wags its tail when it is pleased, puts it down when miserable and up when excited. The cat family lash their tails when they are angry.

Whales, which are mammals living in the water, have developed their tails into fish-tails. There is a great variety of different tails for different purposes, but when they are not used they become very small, as the pig's has done.

SPIDER
MONKEY

GREY SQUIRREL

NECKS AND MANES

The very long neck of the giraffe is another example of the way in which animals evolve to suit their conditions of life. The giraffe feeds on leaves, so it has a long neck and long legs to reach the branches of tall trees. Right down the back of this extraordinary neck the giraffe has a short bristly mane, and many other animals have manes growing on the back of the neck—the horse, donkey, zebra and some of the antelopes. The zebra's mane matches its stripes.

There is another kind of mane which grows like a thick collar of fur right round the neck, and protects the throat from the jaws of an enemy in a fight. The best known mane of this kind is the lion's, a magnificent thick mane worthy of the 'king of beasts'. It is only the male lion which has a mane, the lioness has none at all.

The males of the American bison and the European buffalo have complete manes, which look even larger than they are because these great bulls have thick necks and huge shoulders under their manes.

Wolves, foxes and some dogs have manes which are thick ruffs of fur round their necks, to protect their throats from an enemy's teeth.

LION — SHOWING MANE

LIONESS — NO MANE

COATS AND CAMOUFLAGE

We wear jerseys and thick coats in cold weather, and light clothes in the summer. For the same reason bears, arctic foxes and arctic hares, and musk oxen, which all live in a cold climate, grow thick woolly coats, and animals which live where it is hot have short smooth coats. Some, like the elephant, hippo and rhino have little or no hair growing on their thick skins. Between these extremes are the animals which, more like ourselves, have thick coats for the winter and shed them in the spring. Ponies that live out are sleek in summer and shaggy in the winter.

As well as wearing the appropriate coats for the climate, animals use colour and pattern to make them inconspicuous. Giraffes have dappled patterned coats which look like leaf shadows among the trees. Polar bears which live amid snow have white coats. The giant panda seems to be very conspicuous with its astonishing markings, but it would be difficult to see clearly among the rocks and snow of its home in the Himalayan mountains. The Arctic hare, the Scottish hare and the stoat grow white coats in winter. The bright stripes of the tiger are lost to the eye when it prowls through the dry jungle grass, and the spots of the leopard resemble the broken sunlight among the trees where it hunts. In the same way a tabby cat blends with the background as it hunts in a hedgerow.

POLAR BEAR

GIANT PANDA

TIGER

PRICKLES AND "ARMOUR-PLATE"

Animals either defend themselves with sharp teeth or tusks and fighting spirit, or have long legs and the ability to run away fast. There is another method of defence, however. Some animals have developed their hair or skin into such a strong defensive covering that an enemy cannot get at them.

The hedgehog, which lives wild in Britain, has done this. It is a harmless animal with a long snout, a short tail and a small brain. But it has evolved a very good defence in the sharp spines or spikes which grow over its back. When a hedgehog is alarmed it immediately rolls itself into a tight ball with the sharp prickles sticking out in all directions.

The porcupine has a similar defensive coat of sharp spines, and woe betide any hunter who tries to turn it over with nose or paw. Sometimes a porcupine lashes its tail in anger and the sharp spines fly off like arrows.

Another form of protection is the covering of hard, bony scales evolved by the armadillo. These resemble armour-plating and give the armadillo a prehistoric appearance. The pangolin has hard scales, too, and a long, scaly tail. It is a tree climber and sometimes it curls up and hangs from a tree with its long tail hooked over a branch.

HEDGEHOG

ARMADILLO

PORCUPINE

PANGOLIN

ANIMALS WITH POUCHES

The *marsupials* are all the animals whose females have a pouch in front of the body to carry the young. They have developed in Australasia where they have been cut off from the other mammals in the world for countless centuries. The best known of the marsupials is the kangaroo, which is mentioned on page 30.

Baby kangaroos are very small when they are born; the baby of the largest kinds is only about an inch long at first. It goes at once into its mother's pouch and stays there for about six months until it is big and strong enough to hop out to graze. It hops back again very quickly if it is alarmed.

Kangaroos never walk or run, they always hop with their strong hind legs. The largest kind normally hop about five feet at a time, or when they are in a hurry, they can leap twenty-five feet.

The smaller kinds of kangaroo are called wallabies. Other marsupials are the Tasmanian wolf, the tiger-cat, the bandicoot, which is a burrowing animal like a rabbit, and, the most popular of all, the little koala bear.

The koala bear, which looks like a woolly teddy bear, lives in eucalyptus trees and eats only eucalyptus leaves. The babies leave their mothers' pouches very soon and ride on the backs of their mothers.

The only marsupial found outside Australasia is the opossum of North America. The baby opossum also rides on its mother's back, clinging to the curved-over tail.

KOALA
BEARS

ANGAROOS

OPOSSUMS

SWIMMING MAMMALS

Whales, dolphins and porpoises, which are all members of the whale family, look like fishes and live like fishes, yet they are mammals, because they nourish their young on their mothers' milk. They have adapted themselves completely to life in the sea; their forelegs have become flippers, hind-legs have disappeared and tails have become full fish-tails.

An important difference between the whales and fish is that whales have to come to the surface to breathe. A whale's nostril, or 'blow-hole', is near the top of its head, and has a valve which closes when the whale submerges, so that it is not drowned. When a whale comes up to breathe out, or 'blow', it sends up a fountain of water. Whales are the largest of all the mammals; the common rorqual whale can be eighty feet long.

There is another group of mammals which are as much sea as land creatures: the seal, sealion and walrus. They differ from the whales in that they can live on land as well as in the water, for they breed on the sea-shore and live on fish they catch in the sea. Their limbs are fin-shaped and they swim like fish. They look clumsy ashore, but they can move quickly.

The otter is another mammal which has adapted itself to a life in the water, usually rivers. It looks like a seal, it swims easily, it lives on fish but at the same time it can run very fast on land. The otter is really a land animal adapted for swimming, and helped by having webbed feet.

WHALE BLOWING

SEAL

OTTER

FLYING MAMMALS

As whales and seals have adapted themselves to a fish-like life, so are there mammals which have become more like birds than animals. These are the bats, which are flying mammals.

A bat's 'wings' are quite different from a bird's; they are webbed arms, like the webbed feet of the swimming mammals. Arm and hand is elongated and joined to the furry mouse-like body with a membrane of skin. By beating its arms quickly and cleverly a bat can fly as well as any feathered bird as it chases the insects which are its food. Some tropical bats, however, eat fruit.

People sometimes use the expression 'as blind as a bat'. But bats are not blind. Because they live mostly in dark caves or buildings, and only fly out to feed at night, they do not need to use their eyes.

Instead of using their eyes bats have developed a wonderful system like radar. A bat makes a high-pitched squeak as it flies, a note too high for most human ears to hear. This sound echoes off any object in the way and the creature is warned in time to avoid it. Scientists have observed bats flying in a pitch dark room with many thin wires stretched across, and thanks to the radar system, they have not touched a single wire.

Bats are strange and interesting animals. They sleep hanging upside down with their 'wings' wrapped around their bodies.

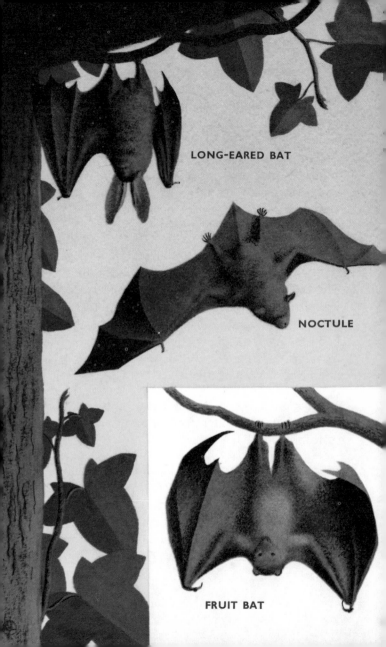

LONG-EARED BAT

NOCTULE

FRUIT BAT

HIBERNATION AND STORING FOOD

Hibernation means the 'winter sleep' of some animals. When an animal's natural food cannot be obtained during the winter it has evolved a system by which it can survive without eating. It eats a lot while food is still plentiful, and becomes very fat. Then it finds a quiet and safe place and goes to sleep. Its heart-beats and breathing slow down and it sleeps away the winter months, living on the fat already stored in the body. In the spring it emerges, thin and scraggy, but soon feeds itself up again.

Different animals go into different depths of hibernation. The dormouse sleeps profoundly all the time. The bear sleeps most of the time but less deeply and wakes up occasionally. In fact the mother bear has her cubs during the hibernation period. Hedgehogs, badgers and bats hibernate, but they sometimes go foraging on a winter's night, and then go back for another long spell of sleep.

Other animals, like the squirrel with its hoard of nuts, prepare for the winter food shortage by laying in a store.

Camels travelling across a desert often have to go without food or water for a number of days, so they store emergency supplies in their humps. The single hump of the dromedary or Arabian camel, and the double humps of the Bactrian camel, are stores of fat which can be absorbed as food and drink when necessary.

CAMELS IN THE DESERT

ENTRANCE
TO SETT

OLD CHAMBERS
OF PREVIOUS YEAR

HEAP OF EARTH
ND OLD BEDDING

BREEDING CHAMBER
LINED WITH DRY BRACKEN
AND HAY

TO SECOND
ENTRANCE

HIBERNATING
BADGER IN
SLEEPING CHAMBER

HOME-MAKING

Mammals which live in large groups, such as herds of deer, do not need a home of their own. Some animals are solitary and have their independent family life and make a home. Others are neighbourly, like rabbits, with many families living in their own homes in a large warren, or beavers in their lodges.

The beaver's lodge is a wonderful achievement of building and engineering. A colony of beavers will spend much time and energy building a dam across the stream where they want to live, because they must have fairly deep water. They fell trees by gnawing them with their sharp rodent teeth, and drag or float them to the site to be fixed in position. When the main structure is finished it is filled in with brushwood, stones and mud. Beavers can build a dam twelve feet high and a hundred feet across.

When the dam is finished and the water is the right depth they build their own homes, making islands in the deep water, surrounding them with walls and topping them with a dome of sticks and mud. When the mud freezes in the winter, as it always does in Canada and northern Europe where the beavers live, the lodge becomes very strong and warm inside. The entrances are holes under the water, and therefore safe from enemies.

The underground earths of foxes and setts of badgers have more than one entrance. Gorillas build a nest in trees with a platform of branches and knotted creepers.

DAM

TOP OF BEAVER'S LODGE
ABOVE FROZEN SURFACE
OF STREAM

UNDERWATER ICE FREE
ENTRANCE TO LODGE

INSTINCT AND KNOWLEDGE

An animal behaves to a certain extent by instinct. This is a sense, or knowledge, to act in a certain way because an animal's ancestors have done it for many generations. A dog will bark at a strange sound by instinct. If an animal falls into water accidentally it will swim to the shore, even if it has not been taught to swim. It knows what to do by its instinct for survival.

But some animals are taught to swim. An otter will swim out to deep water with its baby on its back and then dive, so that the baby has to swim back. It does this time after time until the young otter gains confidence, and learns to enjoy swimming. This is knowledge, the result of education, and not instinct.

The young have to be educated, just as we are sent to school to learn how to do things. A cat teaches her kittens to hunt by making them chase the tip of her tail in play. Then she will give them a mouse and show them what to do. Lions and tigers teach their cubs to hunt; it is an essential lesson in the wild if they are not to starve.

Young animals have to be taught to be independent, to add knowledge and skill to their natural instincts. A mother bear teaches her cubs to stay with her, to remain quiet and to hunt, and if they are disobedient she picks them up and spanks them—hard.

BEAR WITH CUBS

HAND AND BRAIN

Many animals use their front paws like hands. A squirrel or a hamster will hold a nut in its front paws, and a dog holds down a bone while gnawing it, and so do lions and tigers. A kangaroo will use its dainty fore-feet to hold leaves it is eating or to scratch its stomach. Moles and badgers use their 'hands' for digging, a monkey uses its hands, and feet, all the time.

It is the co-ordination of hand and brain, the way they are used together, which is the mark of intelligence. The top order of the mammals is called the *primates,* and includes monkeys, apes and Man. These have the most highly developed hands which they use in varying degrees under the direction of the brain.

The apes—chimpanzees, gorillas and orang-outangs, which are Man's nearest cousins in the animal kingdom, have remarkable co-ordination between brain and hand. A chimpanzee will put one box on top of another to climb up something. It has been known to join two sticks together to make a longer one and reach fruit. Apes in the wild state have been seen using bunches of leaves like sponges, to soak up water from a difficult place, and then squeezing it into their mouths.

Intelligence depends on using the brain to think and reason, instead of relying only on natural instincts.

HAMSTER WITH NUT

CHIMPANZEE SQUEEZING
WATER FROM LEAF-SPONGE

SIMPLIFIED ORDER OF MAMMALS

Page numbers are given for mammals included in this book.
Heavy type denotes illustrations.